Feeling Good
About
Feeling Bad

Feeling Good About Feeling Bad

PAUL L. WARNER
with Sam Crabtree, Jr.

WORD BOOKS
PUBLISHER
WACO, TEXAS

FEELING GOOD ABOUT FEELING BAD

ISBN 0–8499–0104–9
Library of Congress catalog number: 78–59431
Printed in the United States of America

Scripture quotations marked KJV are from the King James Version of the Bible.

Scripture quotations marked TLB are taken from *The Living Bible, Paraphrased* (Wheaton: Tyndale House Publishers, 1971) and are used by permission.

Scripture quotations marked NAS are taken from *The New American Standard Bible* copyright © The Lockman Foundation 1960, 1962, 1963, 1968, 1971.

The article "Fireworks in Reverse" is reprinted by permission from *Campus Life* magazine, copyright © 1970, Youth for Christ International, Wheaton, Illinois.

Grateful acknowledgment is made for permission to quote from Robert Raines's *To Kiss the Joy*, Word Books Publishers, © 1973 by Word, Incorporated, Waco, Texas.

Cartoons and illustrations are by Sam Crabtree, Jr.

To
my wife and family

Contents

Introduction

VERY SOON AFTER I began the practice of psychiatry, various groups asked me to come speak to them and share with them the ideas that I had with regard to psychiatry and how it fits in with the teachings of Christianity. On many of these occasions people would ask if the material which was presented in the talks was in written form, but I was unable to refer them to a source that contained the things that had been presented. Now, after several years of prodding by friends, my wife and most recently the members of the Dynalife Christian Ministries, these ideas are finally being put down on paper; and the following chapters contain the concepts which I have developed over the years both in the practice of psychiatry and of general medicine.

The stimulus for this work came from questions which were problems to me during teen-age and young adult life when I worked as a plasterer, spent three years in military service during World War II and attended college. I was troubled by such questions as, "Why do I feel a sense of shame about things that other people do not seem to be ashamed of?" and "Why do I experience a sense of guilt at thoughts and feelings which I cannot help but have?" For example, being brought up in a strong prohibition environment, I ended up sensing guilt at even the smell of beer or liquor. There were times that I would become guilt-ridden when a temptation thought would come to my mind.

The concepts which follow have helped me in answering these questions, and it is my hope that they will be of help to many who read the material shared in these pages.

Many people, including my parents, many teachers, pastors and friends, have had a part in preparing me to write this book. To each one I am grateful.

My special thanks to Sam Crabtree, Jr. whose assistance in helping organize and write some of the material was invaluable.

I.

Feeling Bad
About Feeling Bad

NO PARENT GETS out of bed in the morning intending
to make his family life unbearable. No mother says to
herself, "Today I will nag, yell, and humiliate my
family whenever possible." No father vows that "today I will provoke my wife and beat my kids." No
teenager determines to "smart off as much as I can,
and blow my temper, and feel bumped out all day."
On the contrary. In the morning many resolve: "This
is going to be a peaceful day. No yelling, no arguing,
and no fighting." Yet, in spite of good intentions, the
unwanted war breaks out again. Once again we find
ourselves saying things we do not mean, in a tone we
do not like, and feeling just lousy about the whole
thing.

In the title of this chapter, I have used the word
feeling incorrectly on purpose because it is commonly
misused that way in our culture. A correct title gram-
matically might be "On Being Guilty about Feeling
Bad."

Certainly no one sets about trying to make children

11

feel guilty about how they look, or guilty that they are either a boy or a girl, or guilty that they have feelings. In spite of the fact that we do not *plan* to develop guilt attitudes about ourselves, most of us end up sooner or later feeling guilty about some things that we should not have to feel guilty about.

In my childhood I was present at many evangelistic meetings, and it was common to see people go to the altar seeking forgiveness over and over again but come away without the relief they were seeking. These people, for the most part, were seeking forgiveness for things which they weren't guilty of in the first place. So it was impossible to get forgiveness.

However, many people who went to the altar *did* come away with relief. These people had come confessing *real* offenses and had experienced the forgiveness of God. Forgiveness brought them relief because they actually were guilty.

However, the people who went away without relief were laboring under the false belief that something about their bodies, or emotions, or temptation thoughts was wrong or sinful and had to be confessed. But our bodies are natural. Our emotions are a very normal part of us all. Temptation thoughts, too, are natural. We can't get rid of our bodies, emotions, or temptations. So people who feel guilty about their bodies or emotions or temptations are doomed to failure in seeking relief because it's impossible to get rid of them. If they could understand this correctly, they would see that the very thing that they feel guilty about is the very thing that makes us wonderfully human, that identifies us with each other, and identifies us with Christ.

Frequently people tell me about feeling embarrassed or shy around certain people, and for no apparent reason. They tell me that they have resolved not to be embarrassed around those people any more, but (lo and behold!) they experience that same feeling again anyway. As a result of these reoccurring feelings they often become frustrated, angry, or depressed. They end up thinking that something is wrong with themselves and "feeling bad about feeling bad."

During military life there were times when fear was the normal response to the situation at hand. One of my buddies was a fellow who would never admit to fear. He had been taught as a child that it was cowardly to be fearful, and as a result he was very uncomfortable if he thought anyone noticed him when he was scared. He had a problem about feeling fear. He felt bad about feeling fear. You might say he felt bad about feeling bad.

Another young man told me one day that he could never separate hate from anger. Every time he felt anger, he thought it meant he hated the person with whom he was angry. So if his best friend happened to make him angry, he thought that deep down he must really hate his best friend. Obviously this man had a problem with "feeling bad about feeling bad" (feeling bad about feeling anger) .

As a general practitioner in a small rural town in Iowa, I often received patients at the office who said, "Doc, I've had this pain for a while and haven't wanted to tell anyone," or "I hope that you don't find anything wrong, because I'm afraid of having something wrong with me." People with skin rashes or some physical deformity would come with the rash, or lesion, or injury, or sore well concealed because of the shame they felt about being so "deformed." These people had a problem accepting their bodies. They had a problem with feeling bad about physical symptoms.

Many symptoms which are treated in doctors' offices and hospitals have no apparent cause. Some of these undoubtedly arise from yet undiscovered causes, but others are without a doubt the result of deep-seated emotional problems that have been repressed so long and so "well" that the individual is not aware of the original problem any more. These people are in a real sense "feeling bad about feeling bad."

Another way of saying "feeling bad about feeling bad" is irrational guilt. Shame is another word that means just about the same thing, and this irrational guilt or shame can occur in almost any aspect of our life.

A true story was related to me recently about a Sunday School superintendent who was reading the Christmas story as it is recorded in Luke. He was reading from *The Living Bible* in which the word *pregnant* is substituted for *great with child*. After the service in which he had read the account, he asked his pastor if it was all right to read the word *pregnant* in church. The superintendent said he felt funny reading that word in church.

It may very well be good that he was able to verbalize his uneasiness, but the mere existence of this feeling indicates an improper and unhealthy attitude about sex that is evident in some churches. Sex is very natural. It is a normal part of human life. But this man's irrational guilt about sex hindered him from reading the Bible in public.

Oh, yes! There is such a thing as real guilt. When an individual performs a breach of the moral law of God, it needs to be taken care of by God's merciful forgiveness with appropriate punishment according to law.

But in this book we want to look at why we develop *irrational* guilt about the physical, emotional, or psychic aspects of our human existence. And we want to look at how an attitude of irrational guilt can be changed to one of non-guilt.

This state of "non-guilt" would allow one to live with an attitude which would make it possible in any physical, emotional, or psychic state to identify with every other human being, including the humanity of Jesus Christ. Further, any temptation state would result in the same kind of identification. Guilt only occurs in this ideal state when we actually break the rules which we have incorporated into our conscience. If we are a Christian, this means guilt is reserved for any breach of the moral law of God.

According to the doctrine of original sin, it is the will of man that is primarily corrupted, and the body of man suffers along with the corrupt will. But so many people have the notion that the body with its feelings and emotions is bad and reeks with evil. Not so. Perhaps that notion comes from the word *flesh* in the Scriptures, but that's a misinterpretation.

Someone has said that life is a tragedy for those who feel, a comedy for those who think. People need to be able to think—to think of their physical, emotional, and psychic feelings as normal; and also to think that temptation which arises from these natural feelings is normal. No one needs to feel guilty about the natural parts of himself. One needs to experience guilt only when one is indeed actually guilty—guilty of breaking God's moral law.

Irrational guilt is an attitude that can be changed so that we no longer have to "feel bad about feeling bad."

II.

Your Feelings Are You

OURS IS THE AGE in which the relativity of Einstein is considered absolute and the absolutes of the Bible are considered relative. But scientific fact never disagrees with spiritual truth. As more and more is being discovered about our brain and how it functions, the more we see how it correlates with Christian teaching in regard to how we handle our feelings.

These feelings are all a normal, involuntary part of the humanity of each one of us. We can't shut them off. And there is no such thing as an abnormal feeling state. When we feel something, it is as much a normal part of us as the hand on the end of our arm or the nose on our face. Therefore, it is just as wrong to say, "What's the matter with you for having fear?" as it is irrational to say, "What's the matter with you for having a nose on your face?"

Human existence is a dynamic, ever-changing process in which God and his truth is the only unchanging, dependable reality. God's creating and sustaining quality gives us something we can depend upon. Our bodies function according to his plan, his truth. So it follows that, if a scientific truth is discovered about our bodies, it will agree with all other truth—whether physical, spiritual, or any other truth of the cosmos.

One of the parts of the human body about which very little is known is the brain and its functioning. There are some things we do know, however, and it is interesting to see how they correlate with Christian teaching.

As shown in the diagrammatic sketch of the brain on page 19, there is a voluntary area of our brain and an involuntary part of our brain. There are many connecting fibers between these two areas, and the whole brain functions on an electrical-chemical basis. It is like a whole bunch of telephone lines running from the involuntary part of the brain to the voluntary part of the brain. Down in the center or the base of our brain is a group· of small nerve centers which are the source of our feelings. These feelings are instinctual responses to any stimulus whether it be from an external source or from an internal source such as memory. When one of these nerve centers receives a stimulus, it makes a phone call to the voluntary part of the brain. That is when we realize we are experiencing a feeling. Subconsciously we hear the phone ringing in the voluntary part of the brain.

The way I am using the word *feelings* applies only to these instinctual, automatic responses which are part of man's experience. I'm referring only to those little phone calls that are made by the nerve centers when they receive stimulation. I am *not* referring to opinions which we hold on various subjects.

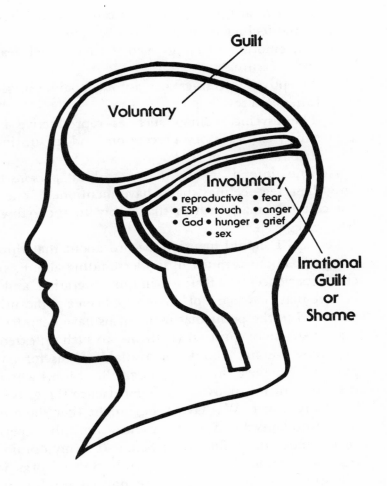

As you look at the diagram, you can see that I have
divided the feeling states into three groups:

1. The emotional feelings such as anger, grief, fear,
   and pleasure.
2. The physical feelings such as touch, pain, hunger,
   thirst, and sex.
3. The psychic feelings such as reproductive in-
   stinct, extra-sensory perception, and an instinctual awareness of God.

I do not intend, by any means, to limit persons to
only these few feelings that I have mentioned. There
are certainly many others that apply to these three
basic categories.

Perhaps I should mention a word about that third
category. There is much misunderstanding about psychic experiences and feelings in our generation, and I
believe that very many of them have been significantly
repressed to the point that many of us have deep feelings of shame or guilt about them—to such an extent
that they are just about not available to us for any
purpose. I believe this to be one of the reasons why it
is so difficult for many of us to experience the gifts of
the Holy Spirit. We have been taught that some of
the natural psychic-type experiences are only experienced under the influence of Satan. It is my opinion
that one of the ways that the Holy Spirit works in
Christian people is through the normal psychic, involuntary part of the brain. I believe this is the way
God made us. Satan is only pleased when he can keep
us believing the lie about ourselves that our psychic
abilities are his entire domain. Satan would have us

believe that all psychic phenomena are automatically
evil. I don't believe that.

If you check up on the person who says life isn't
worth living, you will most likely find that the life he
lives isn't.

Perhaps you don't feel that your life is a candidate
for the "Abundant Life of the Year Award." Maybe it
seems to you that you're on a treadmill—too much
static, same old routine. And it makes you frustrated,
angry, or depressed. The real problem is what to do
about the anger and frustration. Swallow it? Let it boil
inside? Or what? And if it should be taken out, on
whom should you take it out? How should you handle
those little phone calls from the involuntary part of
the brain?

One of the assets of being a human is having the op-
tion of changing whatever situation presents itself. And
if the situation cannot be changed, then one's attitude
toward the situation can be changed. So you can either
look on the bright side; or if you can't see the bright
side, polish the dull side. If the grass on the other side
is greener, maybe your own needs fertilizer.

We *can* change our way of living, and this book is
based on that premise. My psychiatric practice is based
on that premise. There *is* hope. Bad situations can be
made better. Problems have solutions. We *can* deal
with our feelings.

The tremendous adventure of developing from an
infant to an adult is sometimes made hazardous by a
misconception—a misconception about oneself which
leaves him perplexed about whether or not what he

experiences is really a part of himself. (Was I angry for just a minute, or am I an "angry-type person"?) When one is uncertain about whether or not what he feels is really a part of himself, he can develop mental or emotional symptoms for which he may have to seek help in a counselor's office.

The problem of knowing what is really an acceptable part of us is almost universal in our culture and is not foreign to Christians. As a matter of fact, misinterpretation of Christian doctrine is probably one of the main sources of guilt feelings or shame. When someone experiences shame about some physical or emotional part of himself, it is easy for him to get the impression of himself that he is different from other people or weird.

Oh, sure, everyone *is* different from everyone else in the sense of being a unique, one-of-a-kind, special human being. And that's a positive sense of uniqueness. But it's not positive at all to consider oneself weird or to feel guilty about some part of himself.

To feel guilt or shame about our bodies or some part of our emotional lives is one of the lies that the Devil wants us to keep on believing because it is the very thing which keeps us from being able to identify with Christ in his humanity. The solution to this misconception is to understand more correctly the nature of our own humanity as we are identified with the humanity of Jesus Christ.

Feeling states, such as anger, grief, pleasure, fear, and all of the physical feelings, are a normal part of the humanity of each one of us. There is no such thing as an abnormal feeling state. For emphasis, let me repeat that. There is no such thing as an abnormal feel-

ing state. When you feel something, it is as much a
normal part of you as the nose on your face or the
hand on the end of your arm. I believe this to be true
no matter what caused the feeling that the individual
might be having.

Look again at the diagram. Those feelings are normal. If you have a healthy brain and body, then you
will by your very humanness experience those feelings.
You *will* receive phone calls from those nerve centers.

So you say, "Why don't I just have the phone ripped
out? Then I won't get any more of those pesky calls."
Yes, brain surgery is possible but only at the expense of
becoming a vegetable; then not even the good calls
get through. For just as with real telephones many of
these brain phone calls can provide joy.

My assumption is that it is better to be a human
than a vegetable, and a natural, healthy part of humanness is having these feeling states.

In these feeling states we can identify with Jesus,
for the Scriptures describe him as having experienced
anger (John 2:15), grief (Mark 3:5; Matt. 26:38;
John 11:35), fear (Mark 14:36), and pain (1 Pet.
2:23). One of Christ's responsibilities as God incarnate
was to face these feelings as a human. One doesn't have
to feel abnormal when he feels fear or grief or anger,
for they are normal to all human beings. One thing
the discovery of the north pole proved is that there's
no one sitting on top of the world. . . . We all experience "bad" feelings.

In addition to being identified with Jesus Christ in
all of our feeling states, we are also identified with him
in the experience of temptation. The Scriptures teach

clearly in the gospels (Matt. 4:1–11) as well as in the epistles of Paul (Heb. 2:18; 4:15) that Jesus was tempted in every point as we are, yet without sin. It would appear then, that temptations which we experience identify us with Jesus Christ rather than make us different from him as some of us have been made to feel in our childhood.

When Satan, who works through our sinful nature, suggests to us that we should react to some of our feeling states in an immoral or unethical way, we are experiencing temptation. And this is not wrong, not abnormal, not sin. It is evident to us that the possibility of sinning is around, and it is a part of the total picture that results in our realizing that we are sinners. But sin does not occur until we decide to give in to the temptation in our mind, our will, our intellect.

Temptation in any area of life is an experience which identifies us with Christ. He was tempted to lust after power, to give in to hunger, to misuse anger (Matt. 4:1–11).

Many people whom I see in the office are laboring under the false impression that the temptations which they experience mean that there is something wrong with them. For instance, if a person has a temptation to steal, he often believes that this means that he is a thief. I do not believe that this is what it means. It only means that he is a normal human being who has an expected human impulse and resulting temptation. Some people are conditioned more than others to be inclined toward thoughts of theft during their childhood, and I do not believe that this in any way makes them "abnormal."

I believe that identification with Jesus in his temptations is a very important concept and needs much emphasis. When the Scriptures say that he was tempted
in every point just as we are (Heb. 4:15), I believe it
means just that. Any temptation thought that comes
to a man identifies him with the humanity of Jesus
Christ. To emphasize this is just as important as teaching the significance of the divinity of Christ.

A black comedian once said, "No one should ever
be discriminated against because of the 'shape' of his
skin." This statement has profound implications. Just
as one should never have to be ashamed of any part of
his body, one also should not have to be ashamed of
his feelings which result from the stimulation of the
brain. Since Jesus had all of the same feelings that we
have and was without shame or guilt because of them,
it follows that, if we are to be correctly identified with
Christ in his humanity, we can have the same feelings
without an accompanying sense of guilt or shame.

So you see, even though sometimes it is quite normal to be miserable, we don't have to feel miserable
about feeling miserable. In fact, one kind of happiness
is to know exactly at what point to be miserable.

By accepting feelings and temptation without a sense
of guilt or shame, we are learning to identify with our
Lord. In this closer identification with our Lord, we
are allowing the normal functioning of our brains to
help dissipate neurotic symptoms and are producing
a renewing of our minds in a way consistent with the
way that God created us. Thus, we are renewing our
minds in a relationship with God where His Holy Spirit
can do his work more effectively. The Holy Spirit

comforts us by making Jesus Christ real in our lives. When this work is accomplished in us, we are in a stronger position than ever before to resist temptation and live sanctified lives.

With each temptation experience, we must decide whether we are going to give in to that temptation or resist it. Since opinions and decisive acts of the will carry with them the possibility of being a breach of moral law, a sense of guilt may result. But neither feelings nor temptations represent anything immoral and therefore can be spoken of freely without a sense of guilt or shame.

Many of the fellowship groups springing up around the land are helping people to accomplish this kind of guilt-free sharing of feelings. It is also this kind of experience which is the goal of much group therapy in the mental health movement.

In analyzing the nature of man and attempting to explain some of the reasons why our brain works the way it does, I have no intention to attempt to explain away any of the supernatural nature of God. But I see these concepts which God has made possible for us to have as a means of fulfilling the Scriptures as we read them in Romans 12. Here we learn about being transformed by the renewing of our minds that we may prove what is that good, and acceptable, and perfect will of God. I believe this to be extremely important because it is only when we are correctly related to Jesus Christ that we can be effective in having loving relationships with each other and experience what the Scriptures refer to as sanctification.

As we understand the nature of God and the way

he created us, and further understand his acceptance
of us the way we are (in addition to his mercy toward
us), then we are in a position to be accepting other
people and merciful toward them. The development
of this accepting attitude is also helped by meditation
upon the mercy of God.

One of the intentions of this book is to lead to more
Christ-like attitudes in our relationships with each
other. To attain this accepting attitude, an understanding of the *humanity* of Jesus Christ is as important as
insight into the *divinity* of Jesus Christ. God's decision
to allow Christ to lay aside some of the prerogatives
of his divinity and become a human being, just like
each one of us, had a purpose which we must not miss.
A part of this meaning was to assure us that what we
are and what we feel is really "us." My body and all
of its feelings are really me, and I do not need to be
any more ashamed of body and feelings than Christ
was ashamed of his body and feelings.

This incarnation of all of God's power and majesty
into a normal human being is beautifully described
by an article from *Campus Life*:

Shepherds. Stable. Eastern Kings. Peasant's birth.
Why all the fuss? Why the massive celebration two
thousand years later?

A church Bible study group was asked that question.
Various answers were given, but this was the classic:

"Fireworks in reverse."

Think of the grand finale at the big Fourth of July
celebration; the sky erupting with iridescent golds, reds,

silvers, purples and mixed with celebration roars, thunders and explosions. Yet a moment before, all that brilliance was a simple little package.

Incredible: such color and light from a tiny source.

When Jesus Christ came to earth, His grandeur stretched from Milky Way to quasar. He had made everything in the universe: planets, stars, and molecules. All creatures sang, obeyed and rejoiced in Him. It would take a thousand books to describe a small trace of the scope and color and diversity of what He was (and is).

All this He "gave up" to become a babe of human flesh, mortal like you and me. All His power and grandeur focused in Mary's womb.

The Bible tells us "By Him all things consist, cohere, and are held together." Look at trees, snow-capped peaks, yellow birds, blazing sun, music, Apollo rockets. Everything—including each principle by which man built Apollo—was created by Him. All secrets of the universe, all brilliance, all life, pulsate in His being.

All this was contained in Jesus as He entered the world He had made. He was man, yet still God. He funneled down all His glory for our sake, took on man's limitations. Here was God in the flesh, tempted as we are, showing us how to live, then dying on a cross, rising from death to bring us rebels to Himself.

The incarnation: like "fireworks in reverse." Fireworks such as you and I cannot imagine.*

It is not unusual for patients to say to me that they feel that treatment is of no use because they have no purpose in life even when they feel better. Recently a young man of college age suffered a deep depression

*Reprinted by permission from *Campus Life* magazine, Copyright 1970, Youth for Christ International, Wheaton, Illinois.

and was hospitalized following a suicidal gesture. During the initial interview he said to me, "I see no reason to take treatments because even when I feel well, I have no reason to go on." The young man thought so little of himself that he could not see that he was in need of a completely different attitude toward himself before he could find purpose in life. The first step in treatment was to help him express all of his feelings without a sense of guilt or shame and thereby learn that his feelings are really "him."

Are your feelings you? Yes, your feelings are you and they help to identify you with the humanity of Jesus Christ as well as with the rest of the people around you. This confidence is a prerequisite to identifying with the divinity of Christ. As sinners without Christ, our relationship with God is broken. But when we decide to follow Christ, to confess and forsake sin, then God adopts us into that wonderful forever family.

In his book *To Kiss the Joy*, Robert Raines relates the following incident:

> A friend of mine was staying overnight in the home of a Yugoslav pastor and his wife and three boys some time ago. Two of the boys were handsome, strong young men. They were going to the university and showing high promise. The third boy, twenty years old, was over in the corner of the room playing with his toys. My friend asked if he might take a picture of the family, thinking of the parents and the two normal boys. But the father said to him, "Wait a moment until I get him ready." Then the picture was taken with the retarded boy in the center. My friend said to me, "Never show that picture to anyone. We can't exploit human tragedy. But I learned something from that father about what it

means to belong to the family. No child was missing from that picture, not one."

You and I belong to the Father's family. And not one of us is missing from that picture, not one. Each of us feels at times the idiot in himself, feels himself to be ugly, unacceptable, loathsome, outcast. But you and I are in the center of that picture, just as we are, beloved by the Father. Let us feel now that inner power moving in us, like an inner tidal wave singing affirmation, "Yes, I'm with you and for you, I love you. You beautiful idiot, you. You are free now to change and make changes."

III.

Guilt about Being Me

THE NEXT QUESTION I would like to pose is, "Where does the sense of irrational guilt come from?" In infancy and early childhood our nervous system is not completely developed but is growing along with the rest of our body. The nerve endings in the brain have not grown together yet to provide the proper controls over physical functions nor the proper controls over some of the "thinking" part of the brain. These functions gradually develop as the nervous system and the rest of the body continue to grow. Just as a child cannot walk or talk, he cannot think well enough to be able to do any rationalizing early in life. The ability to rationalize, to think in abstract principles, develops gradually as the child matures, and is matured at about the same time as the secondary sex characteristics.

This means that at about twelve years of age most young people are ready for abstract kinds of problems, and we parents had better watch out. From then on they are able to see through some of the irrational ways that adults have treated them, and they become prime prospects for "teen-age rebellion."

During the first part of the early developmental period, the child thinks very concretely. For this reason he may easily develop irrational attitudes toward anything in his life, including his own body and feelings. At this early age, the body and the feeling states make up almost the entire self concept for the child. Therefore, these early developmental years are crucial to the way that he will view himself for the rest of his life. The child cannot see himself as a spiritual being in the same way that you and I as adults can view ourselves as spiritual beings. Let me illustrate why this is true. If I say to you, "You are a liar," you can respond by saying back to me, "That makes me angry with you. You don't know if I am a liar or not." And this would be a healthy response. A child below about six years of age could not respond this way. Instead, he would respond by thinking, "I am a liar—this man expects me to tell lies." This statement would be putting a positive expectation on the child to go on lying.

The same type of response would be elicited to any statement which is directed at the child when he shows a feeling. For instance, an adult says to a child, "What's the matter with you for being angry with me? I am your teacher and only trying to help you," or "Why are you feeling afraid? You shouldn't be afraid—Jesus is with us." Statements such as these teach the child that there is something wrong with him for having a feeling when he could not help but have that very feeling. He is being made to feel ashamed of a normal, healthy feeling. It teaches him to have irrational guilt about the anger that he was feeling or the fear that he experienced. If you will recall the illustration of the telephone in the brain, it is like telling a child that his phone isn't ringing when he can hear it plainly.

The more correct way to handle each of these situations would have been to say, "I'll bet you do feel angry at what happened, but let's be friends anyway," or "It is frightening to be away from your parents for the first time, but let's tell a story and see how soon you can get over that fear." The principle here is to always be accepting of a child's feelings but directive with what he *does* with his feelings. In this way we train him to have good feelings rather than train him to have bad feelings, as in the previous statements. If a child is angry and kicks or spits, the correct attitude would be to say, "Look, it's all right to be angry with me, but you cannot kick or spit at me when you are angry." Then it would be appropriate to give whatever punishment is in order for this type of misbehavior.

A child can be made to feel ashamed of feeling pleasure also. Statements ridiculing a child when he laughs or giggles can make him have the irrational attitude that there is something wrong with him for feeling pleasure at the set of circumstances which resulted in that particular feeling. The way to avoid irrational guilt would be to say to the child that it was all right for him to feel like laughing or giggling but that under the circumstances we expect him to refrain.

Pleasure should be accepted as a normal, healthy feeling for youngsters, even when they might express it in a rather inappropriate circumstance. Recently I had an adult tell me that he can remember that he

laughed during his father's funeral. He did not remember the reason, but he did remember that he had
been made to feel very ashamed for having expressed
any sense of pleasure under the circumstances. I occasionally see people in my office who are in need of
learning how to experience pleasure without a sense of
guilt or shame. These people have in some way—and
not infrequently because of the incorrect interpre-
tation of Christian doctrine—learned that in their experience it is dangerous to have pleasure feelings. One
of the attitudes that causes this kind of response in people is the teaching that the ultimate in holiness and
perfection is to suffer and be deprived of pleasure. In
a child's mind, this kind of teaching emphasized too
strongly leads him to believe that pleasure feelings are
sinful. Later, as an adult, such a person is very miserable because almost any sense of pleasure causes him
pangs of conscience which are distressing. This might
be the explanation for some people's being miserable
when they are appearing to have fun.

Physical feelings, including sexual feelings, must be
accepted as normal or else they will be associated with
marked feelings of guilt or shame. When a parent ob-
serves a child having some kind of sexual feeling—
such as early attempts at masturbating or peeking
through a crack of the door at somebody of the opposite sex—it is a good time to teach the child that this
is a normal feeling to have, and then direct him in the
appropriate way to *handle* that kind of an experience.
Remarks such as, "Ish, what's the matter with you?
That's no way for a child to be," will produce irrational

guilt which can affect an individual's attitude toward sex for the rest of his life. Many sexual problems in adult life stem from such incorrect attitudes learned in childhood. A correct way to react to a child caught peeking would be, "It is natural to be curious, but this is not the way to satisfy your curiosity." Then, instruct the child about differences between boys and girls and why differences are present. It is also useful to encourage them to ask further questions later on and supply literature which is appropriate for the age.

The body is the most important part of a child's self concept, and his physical feelings are important to him. If he is ridiculed for any of his physical feelings, an incorrect attitude of guilt about his body can develop. The following chart illustrates some typical incorrect statements made to children and lists some better ways to respond to the situation.

Typical Incorrect Statements to Children	More Correct Way to Say These Things to a Child
1. "You shouldn't touch him."	1. "It's all right to feel like touching him, but wait for a better time."
2. "You do not hurt—go play."	2. "I'll bet it does hurt where you got bumped. It will be better after a while."
3. "You just think you're hungry or thirsty."	3. "Even though you are hungry, you will have to wait until mealtime."

4. "There is no bad odor here; you just imagine that."

4. "The odor is different, isn't it?"

5. "Shame on you for mentioning sex."

5. "It is all right to be curious about sex, but wait until the company is gone to talk about it."

Since a child's body is so important to him, it is important to show respect for his body. For this reason, physical abuse should be avoided. The greatest power for good is the power of example, and therefore it is up to the parents to avoid the use of physical violence between each other as well as toward the children. Now this does not mean that spanking cannot be used as a form of punishment. Someone has said that children, like canoes, go in the right direction when they are paddled from the rear. However, spanking should never be used when it is done out of anger. When punishment is given for offensive behavior and it has been made clear to the child that it was all right for him to "feel" like doing what he did, the punishment will be accepted without any harm to the child's self concept.

Directiveness—Permissiveness

The rule for small children is: "Be 100 percent permissive with feelings but directive with what is *done* with feelings." This amount of directiveness will vary with the age until the early teens when a child can be given a great deal of leeway in making his own choices, provided he has learned to be accepting of his own feelings and has identified with some mature morals and ethics which give him a basis for wise decisions. In a theoretical ideal situation, the giving up of directiveness in a child could be as early as the early teenage years. For most of us in our culture, of course, this is much too early. Often we are in need of considerable directive influences into our late teens and sometimes into adult life.

The life of Christ illustrates what we are talking about. The Bible tells us that Christ grew and was subject to his parents. At twelve years of age he was taken to the temple to participate in temple activities. This was the custom of the Jewish people, and God had apparently revealed to them that this was the appropriate age for a child to be able to understand the very abstract nature of God abiding in the temple behind the altar. Also, then they would be able to understand the very abstract concept of the Holy Spirit abiding within the human body.

Teens

In the teen-age years, young people have reached that beautiful age where they can completely see through their parents. It is during this time that there is a very strong need for them to be able to learn to make their own decisions. They are rationalizing away as much irrational guilt as we give them a chance to get rid of during these years. In order to accomplish this and maintain a Christian atmosphere, they have to be allowed to get angry and still feel that they are respecting the person with whom they are angry. Further, it is important for the person with whom they are angry to continue to respect them even though they show anger.

The attempt to make the break can come in many different and sometimes unexpected forms—the boy who has discovered a new way to cut the lawn when he knows his dad wants it done another way, or the daughter who decides that she is going to dry her hose in the closet dripping on some newspaper rather than in the bathtub where her mother wants them. These young people are looking for a chance to hear their parents say to them, "Yes, I understand that you have figured out a different way to do it." Then either let them go ahead and do it that way and find out that it doesn't work; or else insist that they do it the way that you expect it done. But be sure to let them know that it was all right to have tried it the other way.

Parents also have to be willing to take the risk here of being disproven or shown in error, for it may result that the youngster's new way of doing things is better than their way. This would be in contrast to the parent who would reinforce irrational guilt by saying such things as, "What kind of an idiot are you to try to mow the grass that way," or "Can't you see how dumb it is to hang those socks in the closet—that doesn't make any sense at all."   .

The teen-age years are times when healthy doubts must be accepted. Faith can be strengthened by doubting something and then, by looking into it, deciding what you are going to choose to believe. Some of the people who have the deepest and most abiding faith in Christ are individuals who have doubted him the most to begin with. I believe it to be wrong to teach young people that they should not have any temptation to doubt. I agree that the older we get, the less doubt we will entertain; and the more we submit to God and resist Satan, the less he tempts us to doubt. However, during these early years, I believe that the temptation to doubt and giving in to this temptation on occasion is an experience which every Christian goes through. Not so long ago I had a patient come to me who had been told by an evangelist that she was a sinner in need of salvation because she had experienced a temptation to doubt her salvation. She found it almost impossible to believe that what she had experienced was not even sin. You see, she had not actually given in to the temptation.

Understanding that young children have to be approached differently than adults and applying the rule, "Be 100 percent permissive with feelings but directive with what is *done* with the feelings," will go a long way toward helping children grow into adults who will be able to "feel good about feeling bad."

IV.

Dealing with the Process

My APPROACH TO patients includes a threefold process —physical, emotional, and spiritual.

Many symptoms for which people present themselves for help are based in physical disorders. Many illnesses are manifested first of all by some kind of emotional disorder. Such things as hormone imbalances, metabolic disorders such as vitamin deficiencies, and other diseases can result in symptoms which cause great discomfort. It is essential to consider these causes for symptoms since it is unfair to a patient to treat him as if he were simply having a nervous disorder if the basis for it is a physical problem.

A careful history followed by appropriate physical examination and laboratory tests will rule out many of the physical causes of emotional disorders. There are undoubtedly some vitamin and mineral deficiencies which can result in emotional symptoms which cannot be diagnosed by present-day laboratory tests, and these have to be discovered by a very careful dietary history. Many elderly people who live alone and do not eat properly probably get better when they come to the hospital simply because they are fed a more adequate diet.

A good many of the emotional problems, however, result from irrational guilt. Symptoms such as depression, phobic reaction (which is severe panic at something which one normally would not expect to be afraid of, such as closed space or high place), and some psychosomatic problems can be caused by irrational guilt or shame about any of our normal feeling states. Psychosomatic problems are those symptoms which result from emotional upsets and include such things as pain in the stomach, difficult breathing, skin rashes, and many other symptoms.

Irrational guilt is to be distinguished from healthy guilt. Healthy guilt results from the breaking of a moral or ethical law to which one is committed. This can be a breach of his own conscience or it can be breaking the law of the land. It can also be disobedience to the rules of the home or the church. When one willfully disobeys that to which he is committed, then guilt should result; and this is the kind of guilt which can be handled by making appropriate confession and accepting whatever punishment or forgiveness is in order. It is real guilt and needs real forgiveness.

Irrational guilt, on the other hand, is about the same as the word *shame* and the theologic word *condemnation*. Irrational guilt results from being made to feel ashamed of our normal feeling states or the way we look. It can result from an adult's using poor judgment about the way he makes fun of a child who has ears that stick out or a misshapen nose. It also results when children are told that there is something wrong with them for feeling anger or fear or even one of the physical sensations. If a child is told, "You don't hurt —go play," when he is actually experiencing pain, he will possibly have irrational guilt about the type of pain that he is experiencing. Irrational guilt can be isolated to a given feeling state when applied in a very specific sense, such as a child's feeling guilty only about being angry at his mother when he can express anger adequately toward other people. With a rather isolated type of irrational guilt like this, the symptoms resulting from it are usually mild. However, the more feeling states about which a person feels guilty, the more severe his symptoms are apt to be.

Spiritual problems generally come from one or more of several possibilities. They might come from a failure to have made an adequate commitment to Christ in his adult life, or unconfessed sin in Christians, or perhaps an inability to forgive offenses. It is my belief that when I help people uncover a spiritual problem and seek the appropriate solution for it, I am doing them just as much good as when they discover a physical or an emotional problem.

The Bible teaches that God loves us the way he created us. To me this means that there is never any reason for us to feel guilty or ashamed of the way our bodies look, the feelings that take place within our bodies, and the temptation thoughts that come as a result of any feelings which we experience. Further, it would appear to me that all of these things actually help us to identify with Jesus Christ in his humanity rather than give us any reason to feel ashamed or guilty. When looking at ourselves in this healthy way, then it is necessary for us to experience guilt only when we willfully decide to break the moral law of God.

God made us the way we are, and his Word tells us that Jesus was tempted in every point like we are, yet without sin. It would follow, then, that when we identify ourselves—the way we look, the way we feel, and the temptations that we experience—with the humanity of Jesus Christ, we are developing an attitude that will help us to overcome irrational guilt and neurotic symptoms. Later when we talk about paradoxical intention in Chapter VI, the reason for this will become clearer. I would hasten to add here that in attempting to use what knowledge we have about the functioning of the brain and applying it to the spiritual concepts, I do not in any way believe that I am explaining away any of the supernatural nature of God's working in us.

In no way do I want to have anyone misinterpret what I am saying here to mean that I am justifying anything that is sinful. Christian people to whom I explain this concept sometimes become apprehensive at this point because they see it as dangerous to say that temptation is not sin. Accepting temptation thoughts into their thinking seems risky because there is always the danger that they will dwell on the thought and have it become sin. I believe that this is where the work of the Holy Spirit is extremely important to Christian people. Further, I think that the work of the Holy Spirit is hindered unless we do accept the temptation thoughts as being without sin until we willfully give in to them.

John 16:7–11 teaches us that the Holy Spirit came into the world to comfort us but also to convince us of sin, righteousness, and judgment. First of all, the Holy Spirit convinces us that we are sinful by nature and under the influence of Satan until we commit ourselves to God by accepting Jesus Christ as our Lord. The Holy Spirit further convinces us of sinful acts when we find ourselves giving in to temptation during the course of our Christian lives. When we are sensitive to the work of the Holy Spirit—as we should be as Christians—we will immediately recognize this conviction, repent of our sin, and turn from it. The second thing the Holy Spirit does is to convince us of the righteousness of Jesus Christ. When we see the righteousness of Christ as he is portrayed to us by the Holy Spirit through his Scriptures, we see our own selves as unrighteous in comparison. We are then in a position to make appropriate confession of our unrighteousness and to approach God on the basis of the righteousness of Christ. The third thing that the Holy Spirit does is to convince us of the judgment of God that is to come according to the prophetic Scriptures. The Scriptures teach us that all sin will be judged unless it has been forgiven by the atonement of Christ (2 Cor. 5:10–21; Acts 10:42–43).

Feelings and temptation are never sin

I have already suggested that feelings and temptations are not sin, but I want to emphasize it a little further. Anger, for instance, correctly defined, is an instinctual response to something which is offensive to us. Webster says it this way: "strong feelings of displeasure, or emotional excitement induced by strong displeasure." Anger is not sinful—it is just a response to something to which we have been conditioned to react with this type of feeling. A person can be conditioned to respond with anger to almost anything with which he comes in contact. The result of anger can be that a person is tempted to hate, but hate does not become a problem to him that should produce guilt until he gives in to the temptation. No one really hates anyone else until he decides to do it. A person can feel intense anger toward someone and still not hate him. To hate someone means that one has decided that this person should be damned to hell or that one has decided to destroy this person's character by spreading an untrue rumor about him. The same principle as described here with regard to anger applies to every one of the feeling states.

Note the diagram on page 46. Down in the involuntary part of the brain, nerve impulses are sent as a result of stimulation. For example, the nerve impulses (feelings) might be sex or anger, as shown. As the person begins to notice these feelings in himself, he may be tempted to lust or hate. Up to this point the person has *not* committed sin. If he is not thinking properly, he may experience irrational guilt; but he has *no real guilt* at this point. However, if his voluntary brain, which is influenced by Satan through his sinful nature, decides to *act* upon those temptations, then he has real guilt and should feel real guilt.

Recently in my office I talked to a young boy who

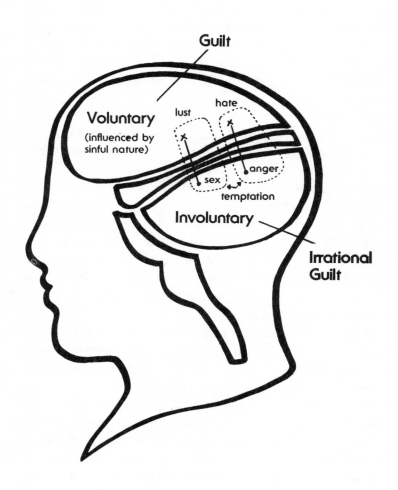

had spent close to five years of his life in a state hospital. He appeared extremely frightened and tense. In the course of the visit I explained the difference between anger and hate to him, and he told me that he had never heard of such a thing. He said he had always related anger to hate and had never been able to separate them in the least. It was gratifying to me to see some response in him to this explanation because I had seen very little response previously.

Two other words which are commonly misused are *sex* and *lust*. Sexual feelings are the normal human response to anything to which a person has been conditioned to respond with erotic feelings. Most people respond with sexual feelings to closeness and tenderness from someone of the opposite sex. Occasionally people are conditioned so they respond with sexual feelings to pain, violence, and almost any object which one can imagine. It is my contention that any sexual feeling from any given source is not sin. Neither is the temptation which may come as a result of the sexual feeling. Sin only occurs when a person experiences lust; and, like hate, lust is an act of the will. One does not lust in a Scriptural sense until he has given in to a sexual temptation. Scripture says, "If a man looks on a woman to lust after her, he has committed adultery with her already in his heart." Since we have established that temptation is not sin, the feelings and thoughts of a sexual nature which occur cannot be sin. Only giving in to the temptation can be wrong. This "giving in" may be nothing more than mental assent, and that is where our sin begins.

Pain can also be the subject of irrational guilt. A

twenty-year-old girl came to me. She had recently almost died of a ruptured appendix because she was unable to tell anyone that she was feeling pain in her abdomen. It was discovered that in her childhood both of her parents, who had thought they were teaching their child the correct way to handle pain, would say to her such things as, "You don't hurt—go play," or "That's nothing—don't pay any attention to it." On two occasions they did this when the child had broken bones—once a collar bone and once a small bone in the leg which they didn't discover for three or four days after the fracture had occurred. As an adult, this girl had to learn how to report internal pain without fear of feeling guilty or ashamed when telling someone how she felt.

In these days when psychic types of experiences are being talked about more openly, it is important for us to look at them and understand as much as we can about this type of experience. I believe that the extrasensory perception experiences within human beings are there because God made us that way. It is this general type of experience that God uses on occasion when ministering to people through his Holy Spirit. It is also this area of our lives which Satan can control and use to confuse us in various ways. It is very likely that children have psychic-type experiences and report them to adults who in turn consider them to be only fantasy. This then distorts the child's view of what a psychic experience is. If a closer study of this whole subject were made, it might be that we could view psychic experiences with much more acceptance as we come to understand how this part of us can be used either by Satan or by the Holy Spirit when we are committed to Christ. It may be that many of us are afraid to accept this kind of experience in ourselves, and thereby we hinder the work of the Holy Spirit within our lives. Just like Peter had to step out by faith on the water when it looked like a completely impossible thing to do, we may need to launch out into this area of our lives with more boldness, being careful that we do so under the guidance of the Holy Spirit with our aim to glorify Jesus Christ as Lord.

In this chapter I have suggested that irrational guilt is the cause of many emotional symptoms. I further suggested that feelings and temptation are never sin, and it is irrational for us to feel guilty about them. This leaves only the act of the will—our giving in to temptation—as a guilt-producing experience in our lives. In the next chapter we will talk about how to deal with sin.

V.

Regeneration

JUST AS SCHNOZ can't expect to be feeling better if he refuses to deal with the medicine, we can't expect to feel relief from spiritual guilt if we don't deal with the medicine—confession and repentance. It's a hard pill to swallow sometimes. But, without it, *real* guilt feelings and conviction of sin won't go away; they are the symptoms of sin which need to be cured by God's forgiveness.

The sooner the medicine, the better, because the

trouble with a little sin is that it won't stay little. Our response to conviction and guilt must be immediate. But, even in the uncomfortable experience of conviction of sin, a Christian need not believe that he is condemned.

Thus far, we have noted that people who have chosen to be committed to Jesus Christ as their Lord can identify with him in every part of their humanity —physically, emotionally, and in their psychic experiences. Also, we are identified with him in every temptation which we experience. One day in my adult Sunday School class we were discussing the subject of identification with Christ, and one of the class members asked the question, "I understand that we are identified with Christ in our feelings and in our temptation, but how about when we commit sin? How does this identify us with Christ?" That's a good question.

In the resulting discussion, the answer soon came out: Jesus Christ experienced the guilt and shame of sinning when he hung upon the cross and took all of our sins. What Christ experienced there on the cross completed the process of identification with us in our humanity and makes it possible for us to be free from guilt or condemnation. This is a significant part of Christian freedom—it makes it possible for us to feel guilty only when we have *unforgiven* sin. We need to be sensitive to the convicting power of the Spirit who condemns us of sin and to make sure that we are not like the man with the clear conscience only because he had a poor memory.

The more I understand this concept of identification with Christ, the more I love people around me and

feel identified with them. It is not unusual for patients
to relate to me some exceedingly unpleasant experiences which they have had and things that they have
done which are even frightening on occasion. Instead
of cringing or acting as if I am rejecting them when
they tell me these things, I am able, instead, to let them
know that I can be accepting of them in spite of their
experiences. The shame that they have gone through
was taken care of by Christ on the cross the same as
the shame of any sin which I have experienced in my
own life. If they are not Christians, I can suggest to
them that Christ has made it possible for them to have
freedom from the guilt and shame of their sins. This
comes, I explain, by being committed to Christ, confessing real guilt before God, repenting, desiring to sin
no more, and acknowledging Jesus Christ as the only
way to receive God's merciful and gracious forgiveness
and complete pardon. For the people who are already
Christians and have sin in their lives, they simply need
to be reminded that God's predetermined forgiveness
is available for them if they make an appropriate confession and then thank God for his forgiveness.

Forgiveness cannot rid one of the irrational guilt or
shame which we talked about earlier, because he hasn't
done anything wrong. He has no *real* guilt to be resolved. Irrational guilt or shame can only be handled
by a change of attitude toward one's feelings or temptations which are behind the sense of irrational guilt.

Another way in which we identify with Christ is
divinity. When we receive the new birth, our bodies
become the temple of the Holy Spirit. Since it is the
purpose of the Holy Spirit to bring honor and glory

to the Lord Jesus Christ, we are then in a position to
have his divine nature show in our relationships with
other people. Further, the Scriptures say in Romans
8:1 (NAS) that "there is therefore now no condemnation to those who are in Christ Jesus, who walk not
after the flesh but after the Spirit." If we are to believe
this, then the Christian who feels condemned in any
way is believing the condemnation of Satan or of self
and not the condemnation of God. This teaching of the
Lord makes it very clear that he did not come to condemn anyone but that he came to save people. I would
hasten to repeat that the Christian *should* feel guilty
when he breaks the moral law of God, and this sense of
guilt will be what motivates him to repentance. Any
unconfessed sin will be judged by the Lord and dealt
with appropriately. We can be sure, however, that God
is not going to condemn us. This is not to excuse any
sin in the life of a Christian because, as the Holy Spirit
manifests the life of Christ within us, he includes the
love of Christ. And if love is felt for our Lord as well
as for other people around us, we are not going to want
to be hurting those whom we love. Therefore, the
more one disobeys God and hurts people, the more
guilt he feels over that sin. But, though he feels guilt,
he is not condemned.

A question which is often asked of me is, "How do
we teach young people to handle sin in their lives
after commitment to Christ?" In answer to this, the
first thing that I frequently do is to find out if there is
an understanding of the difference between the words
judgment and *condemnation*. Jesus made it clear and
Paul also confirms that Jesus did not come into the

world to condemn the world, but that he came to save people (John 3:17; Rom. 5:17–18; 8:1). Condemnation is for the person who refuses to accept Christ as his Lord. Condemnation is final. It is separation from God's mercy and grace. It is damning to very hell. It is God's curse on the total person. Judgment, on the other hand, is not a damnation of the total person but God's response to individual sins in the life of the person. Judgment is God's prerogative, and he has assured us that all sin will be judged if it is not otherwise confessed and forgiven (2 Cor. 5:10; Matt. 7:1–2; Heb. 10:30). Therefore, any sin in one's life—even the life of a Christian—should cause a deep sense of guilt and a fear of judgment, not condemnation. It is a great teaching of the Scriptures that we can pass on to our children that God has provided predetermined forgiveness for all sin, providing we confess it in repentance and thank him for the forgiveness that he has provided.

Irrational Innocence

Sometimes a man with a clear conscience only has a poor memory. A sign in a California department store once read, "Any faulty piece of merchandise will be cheerfully exchanged for another piece of equal quality." It is not unusual for us to believe things about ourselves that are unintentionally deceptive, as was this sign. A patient came to my office with a story of a broken life which had, in part, been caused by a very gross and obvious sin. One of his counselors had dealt with the sin by telling him that it was all right for him to continue in this practice as a part of his Christian life and God would understand.

Many of us have personality characteristics which are very obnoxious and frequently unloving, yet we excuse them by saying, "Well, I can't help it—that's just the way I am." Thus, we go on not feeling guilty when we should. I would suggest that we call this irrational innocence. Similar to the way in which we would attempt to change irrational guilt into freedom from guilt, we should become aware of our sin and try to change irrational innocence into real guilt which can then be handled by making appropriate confession and claiming the forgiveness of God.

A young man who had been under treatment for a number of years was attempting to work out his feelings about his family when he came across the idea that he had hatred for his father. Prior to this time, he had always believed that his attitude toward his father was entirely justified. Although we talked about the angry feelings that he had toward his father and how they were justified and he need not feel condemned about them, he discovered that he had given in to the temptation to hate his father to the point that he had wished his father dead, not only in body but in soul. When he recognized this to be sin and felt guilt about it, he was able to make appropriate confession to God and claim forgiveness.

In this chapter we have talked about sin and how to deal with it. In the next chapter we will be talking about a method which is helpful in changing our attitudes about irrational guilt, a method which I call "paradoxical intention."

VI.

Feeling Good
And Feeling Bad

WE HAVE SAID that there is no such thing as an abnormal feeling and therefore we do not have to feel guilty about feelings. We are now ready to look at a method that makes it possible for us to practice having feelings and to have them properly without all sorts of irrational guilt. We can get out all of those depressed and previously denied feelings which may have been bugging us over the years and learn how to have them without feeling guilty.

There is much that is not known about the nervous system; but, on the other hand, there are some things which are known. For example, it is known that the nervous system operates on electrical-chemical energy. Nerve impulses, those little phone calls in the brain, are transmitted along specific fibers which are very complex. It has been demonstrated in research that one of the main inhibitory influences which is exerted upon the involuntary impulses comes from the voluntary part of the brain. People who have had injury to the voluntary part of their brains from accidents or strokes frequently will have very little control over grief or anger or other impulses because the source of the main inhibition of that impulse has been destroyed. It follows, then, that a person with a normal healthy brain can have control over his feeling states if his attitudes are such that the electrical-chemical impulses are directed over the proper channels. The accompanying diagram suggests that if a person's attitude about anger, for instance, is, "Do not be angry," the electrical-chemical impulses of the voluntary thoughts are directed off into some other part of the brain which does not inhibit anger, and the anger is allowed to come out without any restraint. On the other hand, if the person says to himself, "Be angry—it's all right for me to be angry," and the thought processes are directed toward the involuntary impulse center, then this impulse will be inhibited (paradoxical intention). There are actually inhibitory fibers running from the voluntary brain to the involuntary brain which, when fired, neutralize the anger at the cellular level. This is not the same as repression or denial and does not leave any reservoir of unexpressed energy which can cause problems. It follows, then, that the more we try to have a feeling, the less that feeling will bother us. This principle is true for all of the feeling states including emotions, physical feelings, and psychic feelings.

Let me illustrate how this works for you. Bring to your mind some person or experience in your life which will make you feel angry. Get a good clear picture of this situation until you begin to feel some degree of anger. As you begin to feel angry, then attempt to make the anger more intense. Just say to yourself,

58

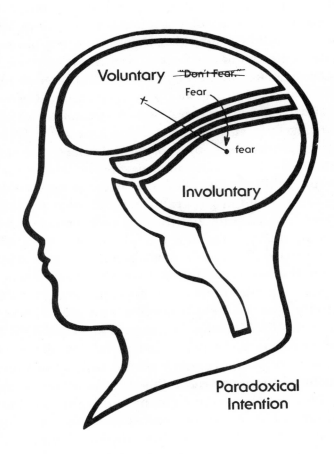

"Come on anger—let's get going now," or "It's all right for me to feel this way." If you will recall for a moment the illustration of the telephone calls in the brain, it would be as though your voluntary brain, the part over which you have control, is answering the phone when it receives a call from the involuntary part. Don't just ignore the phone ringing and hope it goes away; answer! Denying that the phone is ringing doesn't make it go away, and denying that you have various feelings doesn't make them go away either. The more you practice this, the more you will note that the angry feeling becomes less intense. Many times when I do this with people in the office or when speaking to groups, those making the effort end up smiling instead of being angry.

One day in the office I was talking with a married man who had been having some conflicts with his wife; and, when I got to the point in my explanation of how to handle feelings, I explained that it was all right to go ahead and attempt to have anger. He sat back in his chair, heaved a big sigh of relief, and said to me, "I am sure glad to hear you say that. I have been so angry at my wife when she bugs me that I would say to my-self, 'Boy, I'm mad—I'm going to have a "mad" at her right now.'" When he would say this to himself, he did not feel as angry with her. He had self-control. He had previously been afraid to tell people how he handled his feelings because he was afraid that they would think he was crazy. Inadvertently, he had discovered the correct way to handle anger and had been practicing it successfully.

Another patient who came to me was phobic of airplanes. Her husband traveled mostly by plane; and, if she were going to accompany him, she would have to fly. Most of the time she was unable to do this because of her phobia. After an explanation of how to attempt to produce fear as she approached or got into an airplane, she made several trips to the airport to produce fear in herself as she got closer to the airplane. Within two weeks she was able to get on the plane and fly with her husband.

Surprising as it may seem to some, pleasure feelings can be a problem to people. Some of us have gained the impression that there is something wrong with us when we feel pleasure feelings, and frequently this is due to a misinterpretation of Christian doctrine. Children who hear adults imply that the ultimate in holiness is to always suffer can end up with the belief that pleasure is wrong. A frequent complaint from recently married people is that they are unable to enjoy closeness or embracing. Some are not able to enjoy sex either because they have been taught that these things are evil. Their job in therapy is to learn how to have pleasure feelings under appropriate circumstances.

A young woman, typical of patients with this type of a problem, found it impossible to let herself get close to anyone in any kind of a trusting relationship. Her history revealed that on almost every occasion in her life when she had begun to trust someone, he had either died or for some reason had to leave her. She had gained the impression at a very early age that anytime she allowed herself to get close to someone, it resulted in her being hurt by the loss. In therapy we tried to help her learn how to allow herself the pleasure of closeness and a trusting relationship without the fear of rejection and being hurt.

Physical sensations also respond to this "paradoxical intention" form of treatment. Individuals who are extremely sensitive to pain can modify the intensity of their pain by accepting it as a normal variation of human experience and developing an attitude of acceptance toward the pain.

Consider the eastern mystic who lies on a bed of nails; he actually experiences the nails penetrating his skin and stimulating the pain fibers. But his attitude has been so intently concentrated in the direction of allowing the pain to be there and even planning on having the pain that the electrical-chemical result within his brain is that the pain sensation is neutralized and he is able to tolerate this experience without any apparent suffering. It is further my belief that hypnosis probably works in the same way. The hypnotist puts the suggestion into the subconscious mind that it is going to be all right to have the tooth pulled without experiencing pain. This mobilizes all of the inhibitory fibers of the brain, and the result is that the individual does not feel pain when the dentist pulls his tooth.

It is my belief that this method of allowing feelings is compatible with Scriptural teaching. In Ephesians 4:26, for example, we are instructed to be angry yet not sin or let the sun go down on our anger. This suggests that it is normal to have anger, but we should not let it run our lives. Also from the Scriptures we learn that it is normal to grieve over losses in our lives (Eccles. 3:1–8; Mark 3:5; Luke 6:21) and that there are times when we should fear (Matt. 10:28), but we should not let fear rule our lives. Jesus promised in his teachings that there would be times when we would feel good and that the Holy Spirit would be our com- forter; but, on the other hand, he also said that there would be times when, as Christians, we would suffer. The last of the Beatitudes (Matt. 5:11–12) describing the Christian character tells us that we can expect to be persecuted and that if we have the correct attitude, we will be able to rejoice at that persecution instead of cringing under it.

There is no question but what Jesus suffered a great deal in his physical body, especially when he was un- dergoing his trial and subsequent crucifixion. We are told that we are to take up our cross and follow him, and it is certain that many of us may have to suffer in some way physically as a part of our cross-bearing. If we have developed the attitude that we have been talking about in this chapter and in the previous chap- ter, then any suffering that we may have to go through will be much more tolerable.

Group Therapy

Another form of treatment which we use to attempt to modify people's attitudes toward their feeling states is group therapy. It is in group therapy that we pro- vide an opportunity for people to express any feeling that they want to express without feeling shame or guilt at what they say. In the next chapter I will be going into this in more detail when I talk about the rules that we use in family therapy. Hopefully, people learn how to express their feelings in the therapy session so that they don't have to go home and blast their family or neighbors with their feelings and cause a lot of hard feelings or unnecessarily break up friendships. In other words, once they have learned how to express their feelings without guilt or shame, then it is possible for them to choose not to express their feelings on future occasions without its causing them troubles because of a build-up of nervous energy.

In order to identify most completely with Jesus Christ in his humanity, it falls to each Christian to learn how to have feelings—good feelings or bad feelings—and accept them as a normal part of human existence. The more we take this attitude, the more comfortable we will be in our personal lives, family lives, and church lives. In the next chapter we will be making an application of this to family relationships.

VII.

Fighting Can Be Fun

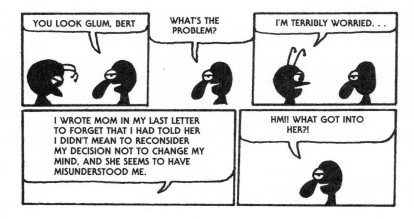

WHEN I TALK WITH young people in my office, it is not unusual for them to report that they have great difficulty talking with their parents and other family members. The only thing which some children and their parents communicate to each other is a head cold. Sometimes, with tears in their eyes, they report that there is nothing they would rather have than satisfactory communication and relationships with their parents. One young man said he wanted this more than he wanted to get off drugs, to get better grades in school, or anything else in his life. Another young man said that, when company stays too long at their house, they just treat them like members of the family and they soon leave.

One of the most heartbreaking experiences that we see is when a person is rejected by the family. This is especially true when a child is not wanted by his parents anymore and for some reason or another has to be placed in an institution or in a foster home. Recently a twelve-year-old boy was hospitalized because of behavior problems, and in the course of the work-up it was found out that his home was totally undesirable for him. When he was about to be discharged and transferred to a state institution, he took hold of the hand of one of the male orderlies at the hospital who had befriended him and said, "I want to stay here with you." The home from which he came was one in which communication had broken down almost totally.

Tears also flow when a husband or wife informs the spouse that they are going to get a divorce. Often too late, they realize that they have not been communicating the kind of messages which help to keep a marriage together. Instead of saying the constructive things and kind remarks, they have been giving in to the old habits of cutting the other person down.

The acting out which we see in children is frequently an abortive attempt to get parents to pay attention to them. The children want to be listened to and understood, and they want their parents to give them the message that they accept them the way they are. When children are not accepted by their parents, or at least when this acceptance is not communicated adequately, young people will frequently act up without even being aware of the reasons they are doing it. The same general principle applies between husband and wife. When love and acceptance are adequately communicated back and forth within the marriage, then there is no need for either partner to seek this experience elsewhere.

I believe that the teachings of Christ put an expectation of change upon each one of us. When Christ said, "Seek ye first the kingdom of God and his righteousness" (Matt. 6:33, KJV), he was teaching us to abandon the human, selfish way of doing things and make a sincere effort to live our lives according to his principles. The old saying which goes, "You can't teach an old dog new tricks," doesn't apply. The Christian philosophy would say, "You *can* teach an old dog new tricks."

During my training period in psychiatry, I learned a set of rules which were primarily intended for use in family therapy. I believe that the application of these rules to each one of our lives as we talk with one another would go a long way toward solving some of our problems. I sometimes call them "Fair Fighting Rules" because they help avoid the dirty way we cut each other down in daily conversation, especially in arguments.

Please keep in mind the principles we have talked about in the earlier chapters as we explain the rules because they make a distinction between our feelings and our opinions. As you will note, the rules apply to our "feelings" and not to opinions.

When properly obeyed, I believe these rules leave each person in the conversation with a sense of respect and dignity that is akin to the attitudes which Christ intended for us to have toward each other. To some people, these rules sound naive and simple as they did to me when I first heard them. Consistent application of these rules in disturbed families, however, proves to be extremely effective in correcting bad habits in the use of ridicule and disrespect.

The rules are as follows:

1. Each person speaks only for his own feelings.
2. Anyone can say anything he wants to say about his own feelings as long as he takes responsibility for the results.
3. No one has to say anything he does not want to say about his own feelings.
4. Absolutely no violence when expressing feelings.
5. Everyone tries to be as honest as possible in reporting his own feelings.

Rule One: Each person speaks only for his own feelings. This rule automatically implies a sense of self-respect since it assumes that the person who is expressing his feelings is the only one who has the right to report and describe what is happening within him. The feeling he is expressing is his own personal private property, and he has property rights upon it. He is in a position to feel no guilt or shame for possessing that particular feeling. Whenever someone else tries to tell him how he is feeling or that he shouldn't be having such a feeling, it is like stealing from him and violating his property rights. The result will be a sense of resentment toward the person who tried to tell him how he should feel.

Anyone who says such things as, "What's the matter with you for being angry with me?", "You should not feel afraid of that," or "You ought to be happy with this kind of a gift," is infringing upon the other person's property rights. The predictable result will be anger on the part of the person being addressed. Rule One also helps us to follow through with the important attitude of always being permissive with the feelings of other people. In other words, we would be developing an attitude that would make it possible for us to accept any feeling that anyone else expresses to us without being critical of that *person* for feeling that way. Now it may be that a great deal of directiveness would be needed in deciding what to do with the feeling being expressed, but the feeling itself would be accepted without question.

If we were to attain completely ideal relationships, it would follow that anyone could report any feeling which he had, along with the resulting ideas about what he was going to do with that feeling, without experiencing any shame or guilt for what he is saying. Sometimes it turns out that what one feels like doing with a feeling would be something which would break his moral code. Therefore it would be a temptation. Too often we feel extremely ashamed for having had a certain temptation and would never think of reporting it to anyone. In an ideal relationship, this would not be the case. In an ideal relationship, where there is no irrational guilt about feelings, the persons may speak about their feelings with flourishing frankness and openness. This helps avoid many, many problems with pent-up feelings.

We must realize that temptations are O. K. Feelings are O. K. They are not abnormal. Having feelings and temptations does not make us into zombies, or even into sinners. Only *acting* immorally makes us sinners.

When people get up enough courage to tell me about some of their secret temptation thoughts while I am conferring with them in the office, I respond by saying to them in a serious tone, "Do you know what that means about you?" Before the patient gets too anxious, I quickly answer: "That means you are a normal person just like everyone else." Often this is followed by an expression of great relief on their part.

Rule Two: Anyone can say anything he wants to about his own feelings as long as he takes responsibility for the results.

Rule Three: No one has to say anything he does not want to say about his own feelings.

The above two rules are best talked about together. By obeying these two rules, we again sense that they give dignity to the individual by making him the only one who has the right to choose whether or not he wants to report something he feels.

The fact that the rules allow a person to choose not to say anything that he does not want to say seems to contradict what some of you might have been taught about the desirability of getting feelings out. Complete freedom of expression has been proposed by some to be a highly desirable thing. I believe that the right to choose what one is going to say is more important than the right to have complete freedom of expression.

It is true that in therapy we must routinely try to encourage people to get feelings expressed outwardly in an atmosphere in which they do not feel guilty or ashamed about expressing that feeling. It is only after they have practiced this in a proper environment and experienced the feeling without guilt or shame that they are in a position to be able to choose not to express that feeling when it would be appropriate to keep it quiet. Oftentimes people are able to express strong feelings about family members or friends while in individual or group therapy, yet it would be highly undesirable for them to express the same feeling directly to that same individual at home. For instance, if a man had some extremely angry feelings toward his mother which he had never been able to face directly before, and when it came time to face these feelings, his mother was elderly, had suffered a stroke, and was living in a nursing home, it obviously would be of no use whatsoever to go there and sound off to her. If he gets this feeling worked out in a therapy situation, then it would be appropriate for him to choose not to express it to his mother. He could go on respecting his mother and treating her with dignity and courtesy so that she could be as comfortable as possible in her debilitated state. Christ made it very clear in his teachings that the loving thing to do is the right thing to do. The man's saving his mother from his angry feelings would give to him an added sense of virtue by being obedient

to God's teaching and sparing his mother this unpleasant experience.

**Rule Four: Absolutely no violence when expressing
feelings.** As in the other rules, this one also implies
dignity and worth for the individual by enforcing
respect for the body. In small children, especially, the
body is about the most important part of their identification as an individual, and to show disrespect for
their bodies by some kind of physical abuse can result
in marked feelings of inferiority as they grow up.
When violence is done with the attitude of shaming, it
can be the beginning of problems in adult life. These
problems can be manifested in such forms of self-
destructive behavior as alcoholism and some forms of
obesity. It could also result in some sexual problems.

This does not mean that I do not believe in appropriate spanking for younger children. I believe that
when punishment is given for offensive behavior, it
will not harm the child as long as it is made clear to
him that it was all right for him to have felt like doing
what he did. Spankings, of course, should never be
given out of anger. Another benefit of obeying Rule
Four is that it gives the person who chooses to follow it
evidence that he has complete control over himself.
When he has a feeling with a resulting temptation
toward some kind of violence and then doesn't do it,
this becomes an ego-building experience. It is very
satisfying for a person to find that, whereas he previously had been allowing his anger to turn into abusive
behavior, now he has control and can treat other people with respect.

A family under treatment was being seen as a result of a teen-age boy who had been involved in delinquent behavior. In the course of therapy it was discovered that the parents were still using shaming methods to attempt to control his behavior. They would write out misdeeds and post them in the kitchen on the bulletin board where everyone, including visitors in the home, could read them. You can imagine the amount of anger which this caused in the boy. His delinquent behavior was a way of acting out this anger rather than taking it out on his father. In the sessions he was able to obey the rules and get his anger expressed at his father. It came out in an expression of rage which was rather frightening; but, since the father was able to obey the rules also and accept the feelings without fighting back, both of them ended up feeling more secure. Soon after this the boy's delinquent behavior stopped.

Sexual attacks on children are almost always associated with shame feelings on the part of the child who is the subject of the attack. A teen-age girl reported that she had been attacked by her brother in her prepubertal years and had been too ashamed to tell anyone. When she found out in therapy that she was not going to be criticized for this, she talked about it freely. As a result she was able to have less depression and suicidal thinking.

Rule Five: Honesty when reporting feelings. Honesty implies respect and worth for both the person being honest and the person to whom the feelings are being expressed. In families where feelings are believed to be bad or children are made to feel ashamed of feelings, the children are put in a position where they almost have to be dishonest in order to avoid being made to feel ashamed. The children can end up being habitually dishonest in the way they report feelings, and later in life they may run into problems because they have not learned how to be honest with other people in expressing their feelings. This can especially create problems in married life. As one reads this, if he looks at himself and recognizes this habitual dishonesty about his feelings, then this is a sign that some change is needed. There is a need to break away from the old pattern of daily living and adopt the honest way which will bring honor to Christ in the believer's life.

It is a real therapeutic challenge to attempt to teach whole families how to communicate honestly about the way they feel. When the lesson is learned by an individual or a family, it is remarkable how much their self-respect improves. Recently a girl, who was hospitalized because of a suicidal gesture, had been unable to be honest with her parents about the way she felt. After twenty years she finally had them come in, and she leveled with them about everything. She told them not only how she felt but also reported some of the very unpleasant things which had happened to her and was very surprised to find that her parents handled it quite well. A much closer relationship developed within that family because of her ability to be honest with them.

I am sure that you can see by this time that the practical application of these principles assists the Christian as he attempts to further his identification with Christ.

The benefits would be noted in his family life, his business life, and his church life. Parents would be more effective in assuming their responsibility to their families. Employers would be better bosses. All human relationships would be improved by careful adherence to these rules. And we would be one step closer to our goal of learning how to feel good about feeling bad.

VIII.

Feelings in the Church

IT HAS BEEN SAID that the greatest and noblest pleasure we can have in this world is to discover new truths; and the next is to shake off old prejudices. No Christian is strong enough to carry a cross and a prejudice at the same time.

We all have our own biases . . . on almost every subject, and especially on spiritual matters. My biases may be different from yours, yours may be different from the next fellow's, and on it goes. The trouble is that sometimes we let our petty differences stand in the way of the multitude of things we have in common. We harbor animosity toward each other because of our differences. We allow our biases to get in the way of really listening and communicating with each other.

Just as we talked earlier about handling feelings in the family, we need also to learn how to handle our feelings in God's family. The Church badly needs to be unified. We need to share with each other, listen to each other, learn from each other. And sometimes our feelings get in the way. Fighting for our position, our belief, our case, doesn't have to divide and destroy Christ's Church. Church relations, like family relations, need to be open and honest; yet like family fighting, Church fighting can be fun, constructive, and productive if the same principles of honesty, self-expression, and nonviolence are kept in mind.

Maturity begins when we're content to feel we're right about something without feeling the necessity to prove someone else wrong. To get up, you needn't knock someone else down. So, when we're asserting an opinion, it is not necessary to make mince meat of the other fellow's. Most people end up fighting for special privileges rather than for equal rights. Sometimes the obstinance or ignorance or stick-in-the-mudness of some people gets on our nerves. And perhaps we begin to feel angry. But we need to be careful that our anger does not close us off from these people.

Possibly the worst thing one can do in declaring an opinion is to close off his mind to the other fellow's side of the issue. Often when we have trouble communicating, it's because we have stopped listening. If we want someone to hear *our* side of the story, it's a good policy to listen to *his*.

Remember the Golden Rule: "The best way to keep from stepping on other people's toes is to put yourself in their shoes." As normal human beings with natural feelings such as anger, you and I both know that sometimes we just don't feel like slipping our feet into someone else's shoes; perhaps we feel more like slipping a fist into his jaw. This is the perfect time to look to God for supernatural help to control a natural feeling and possible temptation to do something a bit nasty. You see, the person who often looks up to God rarely looks down on anyone, and the one who is looking down his nose usually has the wrong slant. Besides, we can't expect a person to see eye to eye with us when we're looking down on him.

Proverbs 13:10 says, "Pride leads to arguments; be humble, take advice and become wise" (TLB). We can't afford to allow pride, that type of pride which is vain, to get the best of us. Pride hides our faults from us but magnifies them to everyone else. Pride is to the character like the attic is to the house: the highest part and generally the most empty. A good point of view preached by a proud man can turn away listeners. A good way to avoid pride is to listen—not just hear, but listen. 2 Timothy 2:24 says, "God's people must not be quarrelsome; they must be gentle, patient teachers of those who are wrong" (TLB).

We've been talking about what to do to avoid stomping on the other fellow's point of view, or even on the other fellow. But what about when we know we're right? What then? Don't we have the right, and maybe even the responsibility, to point out error? This is delicate.

Sometimes it would be easy to burst in zealously, overthrow the tables, and drive out the transgressors. But all too often, those deserving praise the least may need it the most. Those causing trouble may be crying out for understanding, for help, for prayer, for a hand. Perhaps we still haven't listened enough.

One of the most important tasks of the Church is to be redemptive. If people who are down and out, in the wrong, sinners, misguided, or call them what you will

. . . if these people can't find hope in the Church, where can they find it?

Our place is not to judge, to condemn, or to take revenge. Our job is to be forgiving, loving, and redemptive. And sometimes that gets to be a tremendously difficult task. "Turn the other cheek" is a nice thing to say, but a terribly hard thing to do. To love someone, to care for him, to forgive him, to help him after he has wronged us or cheated us or hurt us deeply, requires maximum self-control. We may expect to feel anger, but we must decide to bless. "Bless them which persecute you" (Rom. 12:14, KJV). There's no room for resentment. A coat of forgiveness cannot be worn over a cloak of resentment. Resentment is racing our emotional motor—it wastes valuable energy and gets us nowhere.

Forgiving begins with *deciding* to forgive. A young friend of mine was upset upon hearing of the pregnancy of an unwed high school friend. His first reaction was disappointment, mixed with anger, rejection, and grief. But he made a decision and decided to take a forgiving attitude.

He felt. He felt many things and could have based his actions on those awful feelings. But he didn't. He made a decision. He had already begun to forgive.

On a Monday morning two Christians were discussing what had transpired on the Lord's day. One of them belonged to a very small but legalistic denomination and was overly pious and unduly critical in condemning church members. Finally, he commented, "My father says things are going from bad to worse, even in our own assembly, because yesterday *at least twelve people went forward for the Lord's Supper!"*

"Why would he consider that unspiritual?" inquired the other.

"He feels that many of them were too sinful," replied the first man. "Had they properly examined themselves, he thinks only half of that number would have participated."

"Was he among those who took communion?"

"Yes."

"Well," said the second man, "I don't know about the other eleven, but *your father shouldn't have been one of the twelve.*"

"Why not?"

"Because instead of concentrating on his own sin and thoroughly examining himself, he was passing judgment on fellow believers."

Let everyone sweep in front of his own door and the whole world will be clean. Most of us would get along well if we used the advice we give to others. Kim Joon Gon did just that when the Communists dragged him and his family from their home on Chunnam Island to a spot where 160 people from two villages had gathered to beat the Christians. There Kim's father and wife were beaten to death and Kim was left for dead. When he revived and sought safety at an acquaintance's house, he was turned over to the Communists. Only the sudden appearance of an American ship off the island coast saved him this time, for the Communist soldiers hurried away to battle.

He hid out in the countryside until the South

Korean army captured the island. The Communists who had killed his wife and father were arrested. Because it was wartime, the police chief had authority to execute without trial. But as the chief prepared to kill the men, Kim pleaded, "Spare the men. They were forced to kill." The police chief showed great surprise. "It was your family they killed! Why do you now ask for their lives?" Kim replied quietly, "Because the Lord, Whose I am and Whom I serve, would have me show mercy to them."

The Communists were spared execution because of Kim's plea. News of his action spread among other Communist supporters in the area. When Kim later ascended a mountain to preach to Communists hiding out, he was not killed. Many of the Communists became Christians and when Kim finally left the island, a flourishing church of 108 members was actively witnessing for Christ.

In 1957 he came to Fuller Theological Seminary in California on a scholarship. There he was contacted by Dr. Bill Bright. Eventually he returned to Korea to be Campus Crusade director.

Did Kim feel bad? I'm sure. Grief, anger, fear . . . all in large proportions. But resentment? No. Mercy? Yes.

But that was Kim. Where are you and I? Maybe you and I don't have any Communist soldiers or Hitlers to forgive. But if we really want (and all depends on really wanting) to learn how to forgive, perhaps we had better start with something easier than the Gestapo. We might start with forgiving our husband or wife or children for something they have done or said in the last week. That will probably keep us busy for the moment.

The Christian life is not just our own private affair. If we have been born again into God's family, not only has he become our Father, but every other Christian believer in the world, whatever his nation or denomination, has become our brother or sister in Christ.

A group of my friends who have been encouraging me to write this book were together for an evening of fellowship—there were a couple Presbyterians, a few Baptists, several Evangelical Free folks, a Covenant or two, all well mixed. Now we could have spent the evening debating denominational issues or bickering about doctrinal trivia. Instead, we had the greatest time relaxing in each other as we shared our lives with each other. We were unified in Jesus. We were all born-again believers, unique individual members of God's wonderful forever family.

Sure, we were still different—Baptists, Presbyterians, and so on. God doesn't stamp all of his children out of the same mold like plastic statues. But he molds us all individually using his only begotten Son as the image. We can expect to note differences in various individual Christians. We can count on them. And, indeed, be thankful for them. Who would want a heaven full of robots all identical standing in a line? We must learn to tolerate such trivial differences, even when those differences cross denominational lines. When we are handling our relationships in this way, the result is oneness among the people who are committed to Jesus Christ as Lord. And there is a great need for this today.

There *will* be differences between members of the

same denomination, even the same local church. These differences, too, must be handled lovingly. It is more important to build up each other, pray for each other, and serve each other, than to bicker about what color the candles should be for the next fellowship banquet.

In his book, *Only One Way Left,* George Mcleod tells about the night the Bolsheviks were plotting the Russian revolution. While they discussed the ways to relieve the economic plight of the Russian people, a group of leading Orthodox clergymen was talking about the latest style in vestments to wear in official appearances. The Bolsheviks may have been wrong in thinking that Communism would solve the problems of Russia, but they may have been closer than the clergymen.

The urgency of the day requires that we establish our priorities. We so easily get hung up on trifling little items that the important things go undone.

In 1907 a French lawyer named Maitre Auguste Gilbert asked a government checkroom attendant to check an ordinary wooden toothpick until he called for it. When the attendant refused, claiming it was a practical joke, the lawyer brought suit against the government. The case stayed in the courts for twenty years until the lawyer was proven right. But the costs of the litigation amounting to $40,000 were charged to the government.

Does your church have any toothpicks? Is there an unofficial court case going on in your church? An unsettled dispute? Something that is crumbling the unity?

One day in Africa a small boy was lost. A hue and a cry were raised, but no one had seen the little fellow.

The search went on until nightfall, but no answer came to their urgent calls. The anxiety of the child's mother continued to grow, for she knew that her boy was somewhere out in the darkness where wild animals were constantly on the prowl. At the first signs of daylight, the search continued with renewed energy but still without success. In desperation those taking part in the search returned and held a consultation. Perhaps in their individual efforts they had missed some spot, so the suggestion was made, "Let's all *join hands* and go through the long grass again." Finally the child was found, but it was too late. When the lifeless form of the little one was carried back to the distraught mother, she cried aloud, "Oh, why didn't you join hands before?"

Is that what Jesus is crying out to us today? Are we all running through the tall grass in our own direction? Are we busy forming committees to discuss the latest style of vestments for official appearances?

Let each of us in the body of Christ examine our attitudes to see if we are guilty of making judgments of one another that could cause division and weaken the church, rather than reaching out to one another in love and forgiveness. Also let us not fear the judgment of others which would cause us to be in bondage to them rather than obedient to God. Our minor differences then will not hinder us from working with each other.

Jesus said it the best of all in John 13:35 (NAS): "By this all men will know that you are My disciples, if you have love for one another."

IX.

Feeling Good About Feeling Bad

IN THE PRECEDING chapters, we have looked at suggestions about correcting our attitudes toward ourselves, our bodies, our feelings, temptations, and sin. Life is filled with constant sources of conflict. This is especially true for the Christian since he has taken a definite stand for Christ and is therefore in a position to be in conflict with anyone of a differing opinion. These conflicts are easier to face when our attitudes are geared to accept each conflict and meet it head on.

We are living in an era where everyone is accustomed to dramatic changes. Practicing the development of the new attitudes which we have been talking about can, on occasion, produce dramatic results, but many times the change results from a slow process.

Constant change is an essential part of Christian experience if we are to be a growing, dynamic spiritual being. Our whole body is a dynamic, ever-changing organism. The physical changes in our body, such as chemical changes from stimulants and other food products, temperature changes, and cyclic hormone changes influence the way we feel from time to time. If we have the attitude that any change within our body is bad, and that this means that something is wrong with us, the result is going to be a sense of misery much of the time whenever these changes are occurring within us. If we, on the other hand, understand that the variety of ways that our body can change is just one of the other many dimensions of our interesting and challenging experience as a human being, we can be assured that we will suffer much less than the person who is always striving for the perfectly stable existence. Even the very uncomfortable feelings such as pain, severe grief, and panic can be modified to a more tolerable level by planning on them and accepting them.

Human existence is a dynamic process of continual change in which spiritual truth is the only unchanging, dependable reality. I am firmly convinced that the human mind is capable of experiencing this unchanging reality.

The Scriptures put expectations upon us as Christians which require that we make changes, and I believe that no one is ever too old to start a process of change which will make him a better Christian. It is never too late to change. In other words, you *can* teach an old dog new tricks.

The changed attitude which results in "feeling good about feeling bad" applies only to our feelings, our body, and our temptations and not to what we call sin or sinfulness within ourselves.

When we sin against God, the expected result is that we will "feel bad about acting bad." If we do not experience guilt as a result of sin, we are indulging in *irrational innocence.* "Feeling good about feeling bad" applies only to the process of ridding ourselves of *irrational guilt.*

A number of writers recently, both in religious and secular fields, have emphasized the need for reinforcing a stable family life within our culture. There is much lack of love and respect within families, including many Christian families unfortunately, and I am hopeful that some of the ideas proposed in this book will help the reader to find himself changing in the direction of being a much better family member. By accepting feelings as normal and learning to have temptation along with those feelings without a sense of guilt or shame, we are learning to identify with Jesus Christ our Lord. In this closer identification with our Lord, we are allowing the normal functioning of our brain to help dissipate neurotic symptoms and produce a renewing of our mind in our relationship with God. The result of this renewing is that the Holy Spirit can do his work more effectively. The work of the Holy Spirit in us is to convict of sin, righteousness and judgment, and also to comfort us by making Jesus Christ real in our lives. When this work is accomplished in us, the result is that we are in a stronger position than ever before to resist temptation and to live sanctified lives. This kind of a change is bound to produce better family members.

Change can be very exciting. When we learn to accept and face conflict at the deeper levels of human experience, we are learning what Paul was talking about when he spoke of eating meat instead of drinking milk.

Have you ever been so excited about an upcoming event that you could hardly wait? For example, when you were a little tyke and tomorrow was Christmas, didn't you just about burst at the seams trying to wait? I am experiencing a similar feeling these days, but it isn't looking forward to one event. It is more of an expectation for great things in general—an anticipation for life. I just know some great experiences are ahead, and I can't wait for them to get here.

God is at work through many various projects that I am involved in and other projects that are going on around me, and it's thrilling!

As Christians, we need to share this feeling of excitement with each other. We need to spread the word that things *are* happening, things that make life what it should be: dynamic! A dynamic vitality that stirs the soul. We need to let each other know how God is working in our lives. We need to let each other know what our needs are so that we can pray specifically. And we need to practice being thankful to God, rejoicing in the Lord, and expressing forgiveness to one another. As we get our attitudes straightened around, these experiences become deeper and more vital.

I am convinced that, by accepting Jesus Christ as the one who came to provide complete forgiveness of sin and committing our lives to him, we receive the spiritual power necessary to experience, in the fullest sense, "feeling good about feeling bad."